WISDOM ON...

FRIENDS, DATING, AND RELATIONSHIPS

MARK MATLOCK

WISDOM ON...

FRIENDS, DATING, AND RELATIONSHIPS

ZONDERVAN®

ZONDERVAN.com/
AUTHORTRACKER
follow your favorite authors

youth
specialties

Wisdom On...Friends, Dating, and Relationships
Copyright 2008 by Mark Matlock

Youth Specialties resources, 300 S. Pierce St., El Cajon, CA 92020 are published by Zondervan, 5300 Patterson Ave. SE, Grand Rapids, MI 49530.

Library of Congress Cataloging-in-Publication Data

Matlock, Mark.
  Wisdom on friends, dating, and relationships / by Mark Matlock.
    p. cm.
  ISBN-10: 0-310-27927-5 (pbk.)
  ISBN-13: 978-0-310-27927-3 (pbk.)
  1. Christian teenagers—Conduct of life—Juvenile literature. 2. Chritian
teenagers—Religious life—Juvenile literature. 3. Friendship—Religious
aspects—Christianity—Juvenile literature. 4. Dating (Social
cutom—Religious aspects—Christianity—Juvenile literature. 5.
Interpersonal relations—Religious aspects—Christianity—Juvenile
literature. I. Title.
  BJ1631.M3725 2007
  241'.676—dc22

                                                    2007041817

Cover design by SharpSeven Design
Interior design by David Conn

Printed in the United States of America

08 09 10 11 12 • 16 15 14 13 12 11 10 9 8 7 6 5 4 3 2

This book is for my daughter Skye. As you mature, I hope this book helps you avoid loads of drama. Try to pretend your dad didn't write it.

TABLE OF CONTENTS

I'd like to thank my intern Jill Miller for her help in compiling the case studies in this book and Chris Lyon for providing feedback on this book. I'd also like to thank Jay Howver, Roni Meek and my editor Randy Southern for all the hard work they put into this series.

ACKNOWLEDGMENTS

CHAPTER 1

WHY WE NEED FRIENDS

When I was in sixth grade, my mom and dad took a trip to Hawaii and left me with my friend Ian's family, who lived down the street from us. Ian and I had a blast that first night together, so we concocted a plan to keep the good times rolling, even though the next day was a school day.

Just before bedtime I whispered to Ian, "In the morning, let's fake like we're sick."

Ian shook his head. "No, my mom is pretty sharp," he said. "We'd have to prove to her that we're sick."

"What kind of proof would she need?" I asked.

"She'd need to see us throw up or something like that," he replied.

I nodded. "I can do that!"

I told him the story of how my brother, when he was younger, accidentally gargled fingernail polish remover instead of mouthwash. And then to make matters worse, he swallowed it. My mom drove (she practically flew) to the drugstore to get some syrup of ipecac. Within three or four minutes of drinking the stuff, my brother threw up.

As I related the incident to Ian, I couldn't remember the name of the medicine. But I knew it had a really weird name and we had a bottle of it somewhere in our house.

I laid out the plan for Ian: "We'll run down the street to my house. We'll sneak in through the window and search the medicine cabinet for the bottle. Then we'll take the stuff in the morning, we'll throw up, and we won't have to go to school!"

And that's just what we did. Ian and I sneaked out of his house and made our way down the street to my house. We climbed through a window and headed for the medicine cabinet, where I found a bottle that looked vaguely familiar.

"That's it," I said. "That's what my mom gave my brother. All we have to do is take a couple of swallows in the morning, and we'll be throwing up all over the place. Then we can stay home!"

If I'd grabbed the ipecac, that's probably what would have happened. But instead of ipecac, I actually grabbed a bottle of...laxative.

The next morning, we woke up and went downstairs to eat breakfast. On the way back up to his room, Ian whispered, "Do we take it now?"

"We'll need to take it about five minutes before we want to throw up," I told him.

He nodded. "All right. Let's load up." We each took two big gulps from the bottle. Then we went back downstairs so Ian's mom could witness our sudden violent illness.

Five minutes later...nothing happened. Our plan had failed. Since we had no proof of sickness, Ian's mom took us to school. Unfortunately, that's not the end of the story.

After lunch, I was sitting in class when I felt a strange sensation in my stomach. Incredible rumblings started deep in my digestive system and warned me of bad things to come! I ran to the front of the class and grabbed the bathroom pass. I didn't even ask the teacher for permission before I sprinted out the door and down the hall to the bath-

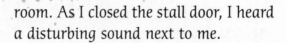

room. As I closed the stall door, I heard a disturbing sound next to me.

"AAAAAAAHHHHHH!!!!!"

I recognized that agonized cry. "Ian, is that you?" I asked.

"Yeah," he moaned. "Hey, Mark, I don't think that stuff we drank makes you throw up."

"You're right," I agreed. "We got the wrong end."

Friends can be wonderful, positive influences in our lives. But as Ian discovered the hard way, friends can also lead us down wrong paths!

That's why choosing the right friends is one of the most important skills we can ever acquire. If we don't learn to choose our friends wisely, we open the door for powerful *negative* influences to invade our lives.

Proverbs 13:20 says, "He who walks with the wise grows wise, but a companion of fools suffers harm."

When I was in high school, I hung out with really smart people. I was only an average student, but five of my friends were the valedictorians for our class. They had identical GPAs. And we had to listen to five valedictory speeches during graduation! (Imagine our joy.)

The fact that I was a friend of such high achievers made me a better student. For example, I sat next to a guy named Steven in science class. He was a science whiz, and perfect scores were par for the course for him. I soon found that sitting next to Steven improved my grades. His passion for doing well rubbed off on me, and I cared a little bit more about how I was doing in class. As his lab partner, I couldn't joke around or goof off because I knew he was a serious student. He wanted to excel, so excelling became important to me when we worked together. Many times, when I couldn't grasp what the teacher was talking about, Steven explained the lesson in a way I could understand.

There's no doubt in my mind that hanging out with Steven made me a better student. And my grades improved a lot...all the way up to a C.

Let's figure out how you can enjoy similar benefits by choosing your friends wisely.

CHAPTER 2

GOD IS RELATIONAL

Friends are a must in everyone's life. For proof of that, we can look to the Creator. God is relational, and he created us to be relational too.

Even more amazing is the fact that God desires to have a relationship with us. Before Adam and Eve disobeyed God, the human race enjoyed a perfect relationship with him. There was no distance, no separation between God and us.

When sin threatened to destroy our relationship with him, God gave us Jesus—God in human flesh—who could relate to us in a human way. And then Jesus died in our place. His perfect life was the only suitable payment for our sins. As a result, sin could no longer separate us from our heavenly Father.

After Jesus rose from the dead and ascended to heaven, God sent the Holy

Spirit to live inside those who believe Jesus' death paid for their sins. The Holy Spirit—God himself—lives in us! How much more relational can God be?

God also made us to relate to each other. In the creation account of Genesis, Adam was made first. Then God declared it wasn't good for man to be alone, and he created Eve. God's instruction for them to be fruitful and multiply (Genesis 1:28) led to the creation of families and communities—the relationships that can sustain us for life. And after Jesus' resurrection, God established the church, a place where believers can offer one another support, encouragement, and love through genuine, committed relationships.

Maybe you've heard the old cliché that Christianity is about relationships, not rules. A quick glance at the Ten Commandments, or any other instructions in Scripture, might make you question that. But look a little closer, and you'll see something remarkable.

When Jesus was asked, "Which is the greatest commandment?" he replied, "Love the Lord your God with all your heart and with all your soul and with all your mind. This is the first and greatest commandment. And the second is like it: 'Love your neighbor as yourself'" (Matthew 22:34-40). Jesus made it clear that keeping God's commands is a way of showing love to God and a way of showing love to others by respecting their lives, their property, and their relationships. In other words, God's rules are about relationships.

In this guide we're going to explore the gamut of relationships—from the most casual acquaintance to the most serious dating partner—and we'll discuss how to make God-honoring choices in *all* of our interpersonal relationships.

CHAPTER 3
THE FRIENDSHIP TRIANGLE

The word *friend* means different things to different people. Some use it to refer to everyone they're friendly with. Others reserve it for only their closest compadres. We can accommodate both groups by using a simple triangle model.

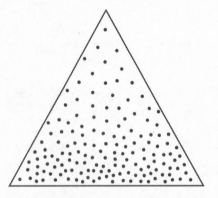

On the wide bottom of the triangle are the zillions (okay, maybe hundreds) of people you know. These are your *acquaintances*, the people you know well enough to make small talk with, but not much more than that. They may include the girl who sits next to you in class or the guy you see in the hall every day. You know these people by name. You may say "hi" to them or catch their eye and give a little nod that says, *Yeah, I'm cool, and you noticed.* But that's about as far as it goes. You don't spend time at their houses. You don't know much about their families. You don't have deep conversations with them. In fact, you don't know a whole lot about them at all.

As you move higher in the triangle, the relationships get more personal and the numbers get smaller. The people in the middle are the ones you hang out with on a regular basis. They may include your youth group, the tennis team, the band, or the people you eat lunch with. You spend a lot of time with these people, and you see each other in good times and in bad. You may feel very comfortable around these people, but the trust level among you isn't high. Chances are, you're often disappointed or annoyed by these people's insensitivities.

The philosopher Aristotle (you remember him, don't you?) called the relationships in this middle level of the triangle "friendship based on utility." That means you have something in common with someone else, and it benefits both of you to get along.

Aristotle also described "friendship based on pleasure." He was referring to relationships that function when people are having a good time together. Friendships based on fun can be a real blast, but they don't last long once the fun stops.

The people at the top of the triangle are your closest and best friends. These people usually hang out in your group of friends, but the chemistry between you is so good that you naturally gravitate toward each other.

Jesus had friends like that. The multitudes that followed him were his acquaintances or the people at the bottom of the triangle. Then in the middle level were his disciples, the ones who were close to him every day. They spent countless hours with Jesus on the road, in the temple, on hillsides, and on lakes and seas.

From that group of 12, Jesus had just a few who were the closest to him: Peter, James, and John. These three were the ones Jesus invited into the room when he raised a little girl from the dead. They went to the top of a mountain with him and watched him talk with Moses and Elijah. They were the ones he asked to stand guard while he prayed before his arrest.

John described himself as "the disciple whom Jesus loved" (John 13:23). That's not to say Jesus didn't love the other disciples; he did. But his friendship with John went deeper. In fact, John developed such a special relationship with the Lord that as Jesus hung on the cross, he asked John to take care of Mary, Jesus' mother. Theirs was a trusting, close friendship.

CHAPTER 4

THE QUALITIES OF A TRUE FRIEND

1 Samuel 20:4,16/7
41,42

You'll notice there's not much room at the top of the friendship triangle. That spot is reserved for only a select few. In my life, God has given me friends who've laughed with me (and sometimes at me), cried with me, listened for hours to whatever I wanted to say, overlooked a lot of stupid things I said and did, and never broke my confidence.

What is it that separates the people at the top from the ones in the middle and at the very bottom of the triangle? On the next few pages, I've listed some "true friend" characteristics.

(I also thought about creating a rating scale for each characteristic so you could give each of your friends a composite score. But then I realized it wouldn't exactly encourage friendship if you said things like, "Well, Jim, you only got a 6.354 on my friendship scale." Or, "Sarah, you ranked a lot higher on my friendship scale than Beth did. Way to go!" So let's drop that idea, okay?)

A TRUE FRIEND IS LOYAL

A few people in my life have earned my complete confidence. I know that no matter what I tell them, they'd never breathe a word of it to anybody if I asked them not to.

Loyalty is one of the chief characteristics of friendship. But loyalty goes way beyond keeping one's mouth shut. Proverbs 18:24 says a true friend "sticks closer than a brother." That means she is committed to you—no matter what. Even if you do something completely stupid, a friend will stand by you.

The 1982 NCAA National Championship game between the Georgetown

Hoyas and the North Carolina Tar Heels is one of the most memorable college basketball games ever played. As the final seconds counted down, a freshman guard named Michael Jordan (yes, *that* Michael Jordan) gave the Tar Heels the lead with a jump shot from the corner.

Now Georgetown had just eight seconds to get off a final and potentially game-winning shot. Out of the corner of his eye, Georgetown guard Fred Brown spotted an open man, and he delivered a perfect pass. Unfortunately for Brown, the open man was James Worthy—who was wearing a North Carolina jersey! Brown's turnover sealed his team's fate, and Georgetown lost the game—and the national championship.

When the final buzzer sounded, John Thompson, the Georgetown coach, made a beeline for Fred Brown. The young player was obviously devastated by what he'd done, but Thompson put his arms around Brown and hugged him for a long, long time. That's loyalty. That's true friendship.

In Ecclesiastes 4:10, Solomon says, "If one falls down, his friend can help him up. But pity the man who falls and has no one to help him up!" We need friends who can help us in tough times. We need friends who will always be there for us. We need friends who will stick closer than a brother—friends like David and Jonathan.

The Old Testament book of 1 Samuel describes one of the most loyal friendships in history—the one between David and Jonathan, King Saul's son. David kills Goliath and saves the nation of Israel, but King Saul becomes jealous of David's newfound popularity. So jealous, in fact, that he wants to have the young warrior killed. Defying his father's orders, Jonathan risks his own life time and again to defend David. Jonathan supports his friend when no one else in the kingdom is willing to help him.

In all of literature, the Bible contains one of the classic descriptions of true friendship: "The soul of Jonathan was knit to the soul of David" (1 Samuel 18:1, NKJV). These two men truly loved each other, and they were prepared to die for each other. That kind of loyalty is sometimes stated, but it's seldom real. Jonathan and David had the real thing.

A TRUE FRIEND IS HONEST

Solomon wrote, "An honest answer is like a kiss on the lips" (Proverbs 24:26). And who better to give us honest answers than our closest friends? Honesty may be the best policy, but it's not always the easiest or most pleasant one. One of the tests of true friendship is whether people are willing to speak the truth to each other and risk a negative reaction.

Solomon also wrote, "Wounds from a friend can be trusted, but an enemy multiplies kisses" (Proverbs 27:6). Sometimes the truth hurts; but when it's a friend telling you the truth, the negative impact is lessened.

On occasion, some of my close friends, including my wife, have had the courage to say to me, "Mark, I really care about you, and I need to tell you something." At that point, I know the bomb bay doors are opening and a bomb is about to drop! I can choose either to value my friend's courage and honesty or to hunker down in my emotional bomb shelter and hope the truth goes away. I don't really like to hear painful truths about myself, but I've learned to value my friends' honesty even more than their praise and encouragement.

A TRUE FRIEND IS FORGIVING

Many years ago, a movie called *Love Story* launched one of the most popular quotes of the early 1970s: "Love means never having to say you're sorry." After careful personal analysis and deep reflection on that quote, I have to say... that's bunk! Love means being *willing* to say you're sorry!

Being a friend means being willing to overlook somebody's bad day. Maybe your friend was rude to you because she just found out that Tony asked somebody else to the dance. Maybe your friend is sulking because he struck out in the last inning with the bases loaded. Friends give friends space to get over whatever is bothering them.

Sometimes, though, a friend's actions will go beyond rudeness or sulking. Sometimes a friend will do something that genuinely offends you. Sometimes a friend's actions will leave you hurt and angry. That's not the time to say to yourself, *Hey, it doesn't really matter. I'll just blow it off.* That's the time to forgive. If you don't forgive—and resolve the underlying problem that led to your being offended—then a wedge will be driven between you and your friend. As more hurts are inflicted, the wedge is driven deeper and deeper until eventually the relationship is shattered. Don't let that happen. True friends are good forgivers.

Paul wrote to the believers in Colossae, "Bear with each other and forgive whatever grievances you may have against one another. Forgive as the Lord forgave you" (Colossians 3:13). Forgiveness isn't a matter of sweeping something under a rug and forgetting about it. When you forgive someone, you acknowledge how hurt you are, but then you choose not to hold the offense against that person.

When you consider the forgiveness you've experienced from Christ, it's likely that you'll be more motivated to forgive other people. That's important to remember because when we're hurt, everything in us cries out for revenge. We desire to hurt the person by gossiping, withdrawing, or attacking. Don't give in to that temptation! A true friend forgives when she's been hurt.

A TRUE FRIEND IS REALISTIC

Friends don't sign up to fill the roles of parents, teachers, or God in our lives. Don't make the mistake of expecting a friend to be anything more than a friend. That kind of expectation puts a tremendous strain on the relationship.

In college, a friend of mine developed friendships with lots of girls. But he was really drawn to one particular girl who was very kind and sweet. He pursued her and tried to spend as much time with her as possible. But I noticed something was wrong: The more he pursued her, the more she backed off.

I knew my friend came from a dysfunctional family. His parents are divorced, and his dad is an alcoholic. As a result, I think he was looking for more than just friendship from this girl. He was hoping she'd fill the hole in his heart—the one his family's hurts had left behind. But that's too much to expect from a friendship! Before long, the girl backed off completely and left him devastated.

Another harsh reality regarding friendship is that sometimes friendships end. One friend moves away. Or she changes her values and lifestyle. Or he starts hanging out with a different crowd. When that happens, the essence of the relationship changes. The thing that made it special—that tied the friends together—is lost. Trying to hold on to a friendship that's run its course is usually more painful than letting it go.

That's not to say a friendship can't survive major obstacles. Many people have continued friendships for years and years despite separation and life changes. I know really old people (like 30!) who stay in touch with their high school buddies even after they've moved away. They enjoy catching up with their distant friends, but they've also developed close friendships in their new hometowns.

There's no such thing as a perfect friendship because there aren't two perfect people to create one. But there are many great friendships we can look to as models for our own—friendships between two people who are loyal to each other, who speak the truth even when it hurts (because they care), who forgive when they've been hurt, who are willing to work through their problems, and who are realistic about their relationship.

CHAPTER 5

WHEN LOOKING FOR CLOSE FRIENDS, WATCH OUT FOR...

Not everyone who claims to be a true friend really is one. If you learn to spot a counterfeit friend before you put your trust in her, you'll save yourself some headaches and heartaches. Watch out for these "non-friend friends":

SHALLOW PEOPLE

Proverbs 18:24 (NIV) says, "A man of many companions may come to ruin, but there is a friend who sticks closer than a brother."

Some people are social butterflies. They have lots of casual or shallow friendships, but no true friends. There's nothing wrong with being popular—unless a person is trying to protect himself from being known and to keep people from getting close to him.

When we try to be friends with everybody, we often compromise our beliefs in order to fit in, and then we end up losing our own values and identity. As a result, we can't enjoy the give-and-take of true friendship. As an old English proverb says, "A friend to all is a friend to none."

My wife is my closest friend. However, I realized that besides her, I didn't have many close friends. While it's probably due to the fact that I travel a lot, that realization still startled me. So I made it a priority to find some close friends—guys who'd encourage me, guys I can challenge to be strong in the Lord, guys I can laugh with.

FOOLS

Proverbs 14:7 says, "Stay away from the foolish, for you will not find knowledge on their lips."

Foolish people don't value the truth about God and his will. They live for the moment, giving little thought to the consequences of their behavior or about anything else. They believe the world revolves around them. They think they know it all, and they believe they should be able to do whatever they want—with no repercussions. In other words, they put themselves in God's position. Stay away from foolish people.

Solomon wrote, "He who walks with the wise grows wise, but a companion of fools suffers harm" (Proverbs 13:20).

Foolish people are often very attractive and enticing. They may seem really smart, funny, flashy, and powerful. However, spending time with them is like playing with fire. Sooner or later, you'll get burned. Find some wise people who love God and are trying to follow him. Develop friendships with those people.

MEAN GIRLS (AND BOYS!)

Proverbs 12:26 says, "A righteous man is cautious in friendship, but the way of the wicked leads them astray."

Wicked people are similar to fools, but their intent is more sinister. Wicked people delight in doing evil. When we use words like *evil* we often picture people who "look evil." But there are plenty of people in our schools and neighborhoods who look normal on the outside, yet they still secretly delight in manipulating people. They use people for their own purposes, and they don't care how it affects others.

The problem is that many mean girls (and boys) put on masks and appear to be very likable and friendly. It's only after we've been around them for a while that we can see what's in their hearts. By that time, it takes a lot of courage to back away from them, knowing the taunts and abuse we'll likely face. Be cautious in your friendships. Stay away from people who laugh when someone is hurt or who delight in doing wrong.

GOSSIPS

Solomon wrote, "A gossip betrays a confidence; so avoid a man [or a woman] who talks too much" (Proverbs 20:19).

Why do some people get such a thrill out of talking about people behind their backs? It's partly because people love secrets. Knowing something that other people don't know gives us a feeling of power. Demonstrating that power by revealing personal information—or speculation—is exciting. What's more, when we put other people down through our gossip, we look good in comparison. However, I believe the main motivation for gossip is revenge—the desire to hurt someone for a real or imagined offense.

If you're a girl, the offense may involve somebody else getting a date with the guy you wanted to go out with. Instead of going on with life, you go to your friends and bad-mouth that girl. It makes you feel better for now; but sooner or later, you'll be the target of someone else's gossip. What goes around, comes around.

Gossip left unchecked is like a virus. It spreads and infects person after person. I see it in high schools (and youth groups) everywhere. One person starts the process, and others join in, continually expanding the hurtful talk. Before long, nobody knows what the truth is anymore! And everyone loses.

Solomon wrote, "Gossips separate close friends" (Proverbs 16:28). Stay away from gossips, and don't be one yourself!

VOLCANOES

Proverbs 22:24–25 says, "Do not make friends with the hot-tempered, do not associate with those who are easily angered, or you may learn their ways and get yourself ensnared."

Do you know people who are explosions waiting to happen? I do. Solomon makes it clear that a friend's angry, short-tempered attitude can rub off on others.

A violent temper isn't something to take lightly. Sooner or later, that anger will be directed at you. That's why it's best to avoid hotheads—people who use their anger to manipulate or intimidate others. If you have a friend like that, have enough respect for yourself to separate yourself from him. If you're concerned about what might happen if you try, talk to your parents, youth pastor, or a trusted adult who can help you.

DEMANDING PEOPLE

Real friends respect each other. They don't whine and sulk when they don't get their way. They don't make demands of you. As your circle of acquaintances grows, you'll find that many people don't know how to be friends. They don't know how to show respect to people. They don't have the skills to resolve problems when they arise. Instead, they try to use the power of yelling, withdrawing, whining, or glaring to get people to do what they want.

All of us can be a bit demanding from time to time, but be careful to avoid people who try to control you. That's not real friendship at all.

FAIR-WEATHER FRIENDS

"A friend loves at all times, and a brother is born for adversity" (Proverbs 17:17).

The test of friendship comes when problems arise. It's easy to laugh and talk and have fun together when things are going well, but a true friend stays close even when things go bad.

Don't be surprised if some of your "good friends" suddenly check out when you need them most. Remember, there are only a few people at the top of the friendship triangle—and all we really need is one. Let the others go. Don't condemn them. They may come back eventually, and they may learn something from the experience. A man once told me, "A true friend is somebody who walks in the door when everybody else is walking out."

Proverbs 25:19 says, "Like a broken tooth or a lame foot is reliance on the unfaithful in a time of trouble."

A friend of mine told me that one of his teeth broke off while he was eating pizza. He had no clue his tooth was brittle; and when it broke, it really hurt him. When someone we trust fails to support us when we need her the most, the pain can be a lot worse than biting into a pizza with a broken tooth!

CHAPTER 6

THE MEASURE OF A FRIEND

So far in this book, we've focused our attention on finding good friends. Remember though, friendships are mutual admiration societies. If we want to find good friends, we have to *be* good friends.

The quality of a person's friendship is a reflection of his character. Below you'll find a list of questions to help you determine your FQ (Friend Quotient). Give yourself a score between 10 (You da best!) and 0 (You da worst!) for each statement.

FRIEND QUOTIENT SURVEY

___ 1. I don't deal in gossip. I keep juicy things to myself.

___ 2. I'm a good listener. I maintain eye contact, and I ask follow-up questions.

___ 3. I'm even-tempered. I don't explode or withdraw when I am upset.

___ 4. I'm happy—not threatened—when other people succeed.

___ 5. I feel sad when other people fail.

___ 6. I have the confidence and skills to be really honest about things that bother me in a relationship. When I'm honest, the problem is usually resolved.

___ 7. I appreciate it when someone is painfully honest with me. I accept an honest opinion graciously.

___ 8. I take appropriate responsibility for my behavior. I'm neither a blame-thrower nor a blame-sponge.

___ 9. One of my strengths is picking the right kinds of friends.

___ 10. I know how to stay away from foolish and wicked people without creating a scene.

What's your total score? The higher the number, the better friend you are.

Now ask your best friends to take the test and rank each statement about you. See if they agree with you about your friendship skills. You can also use these questions to evaluate your friends. (I don't recommend showing them their scores, though.)

CHAPTER 7
DEALING WITH LONELINESS

Few things in this world are worse than loneliness, that feeling of being an outsider. Even the most supportive home environment can't make up for a lack of close friends. Neither can it protect you from the taunts and jibes of other kids at school.

Feelings of isolation can lead to desperation. The desire to feel connected to other people can be overwhelming— not to mention obvious to the people around you. That's why desperate attempts to fit in often backfire, leaving us feeling more alone than ever.

Several factors may contribute to feelings of loneliness and isolation:

· Runaway Emotions—People who have trouble controlling their emotions, especially anger and rage, tend to either push away potential friends or attract the wrong kinds of friends.

· Relocation—One sociologist estimated that 20 percent of all families in the United States move each year. That means one out of every five people has to start over with a new peer group each year. And the struggle is not just for those who've moved. Many people who remain behind experience loneliness because their trusted friends have left them.

· Poor Self-Image—Some people don't expect others to like them because they don't like themselves. They feel as though they have nothing to offer, so they don't even try to make friends.

· Fear—Many people use shyness as an excuse for friendlessness. But what is shyness, except a fear of rejection? If friendlessness seems like a better option than the risk of rejection, it's time to re-evaluate your perspective.

· Poor Communication Skills—Years ago, people sat around and talked during their spare time. They learned the give-and-take of communication and honed their relationship skills. Today, television, video games, and computer time tend to isolate us from others. As a result, many of us haven't developed the kinds of communication skills that attract friends.

Loneliness is an extremely common problem for people of all ages. Everyone feels isolated from time to time. If we don't safeguard against loneliness by building meaningful relationships, we may develop serious problems with our health, behavior, and attitudes.

People who struggle with loneliness for long periods of time can be "eaten alive" by their anxiety. They may develop stomach problems, sleep disturbances, and chronic headaches from the stress of feeling unwanted. Some become dependent on other people as their confidence erodes. Others become violent when their fear and anger explode.

The Bible acknowledges the intense feelings of loneliness. Many of the prophets and psalmists felt very lonely at times. And during Jesus' last hours on earth, he felt the terrible pain of abandonment. But none of us is ever alone. The Scriptures remind us again and again that the Lord sees, understands, and cares about us. He is always with us—even right now. And in one of the most amazing statements in the Bible, Jesus—God who became flesh—called his followers his "friends" (John 15:15).

If you feel lonely, take time to talk to Jesus, the most loving and powerful friend anyone could ever have. Be honest about your feelings. Pour out your heart to him and let him assure you of his love and his plan for your life. Find some people in your school and in your church who really love Jesus and who don't play games to get people to like them. And stop playing those games yourself. Don't worry about social standing. Be yourself. You are loved and accepted by the God of the universe. You don't need to play any games!

Feeling alone can be a very painful experience. But don't let your pain blind you to the friendship opportunities that surround you. Don't forget to be a friend to others. Don't get so wrapped up in your own loneliness that you fail to see another lonely person sitting right next to you! Reach out to others—they're just like you!

CHAPTER 8

DATING, COURTING, AND ARRANGED MARRIAGES

During my sophomore year of college, I traveled to India and stayed there for about eight weeks. My translator was a young man named Daniel, and he and I became good friends during my brief stay. One night I asked Daniel if he had a special someone in his life. He said no, and then he added that he was going to get married in six months. Puzzled, I asked him how that could be.

"My parents are making the arrangements," he replied.

I stared at him in disbelief. Daniel was going to have an arranged marriage. "You're telling me that in six months you're going to marry a woman you've never met before?"

"Yes, the first time I see her will most likely be at our wedding," he explained. "No way!" I said. "How can you do that?"

His response was amazing. "You in the West talk about 'falling' in love, as though it were a downward experience," Daniel said. "Marriage for you is an end. For me, it will be the beginning. I trust my parents. They know who will make a good wife for me. We will rise in our love together."

His words sounded unbelievable, but they made sense. Would you trust your mom and dad to choose your life partner? Perhaps not. But in a sense, we all need help and direction from our heavenly Father to help us find the right person.

Before I went off to college, I attended a "computer dance." If you're not familiar with the concept, here's how it works. Before the dance, participants fill out surveys. The results are fed into a computer that pairs each person with his or her "best match." When you arrive at the event, you're given a numbered nametag, and you're to find the person with the same number and dance at least once with him or her. After I received my number, I searched the room and eventually found the person the computer had chosen for me—the school librarian. Great.

While I didn't appreciate the results of my computer dance experience, I liked how easy it was to find the one who'd been chosen for me. What if God gave all of us numbers at birth and then all we had to do to find his best match for us was simply find the person with the matching number? Wouldn't that be easy?

While God hasn't revealed "exact matches" for us, he's given us principles to use in our search. The principles for girls are a little different from the ones for guys, so I'll detail them separately.

First let's acknowledge that God is in control of our relationships. That's especially important to understand when relationships begin and when they end. 1 Peter 5:6-7 says, "Humble yourselves, therefore, under God's mighty hand, that he may lift you up in due time. Cast all your anxiety on him because he cares for you." Do you trust God to help you find the right person at the right time? If you do, you can relax in the knowledge that he cares for you and knows your needs.

Some people mistakenly believe that if they trust God to help them find their mates, then he's going to disappoint them by providing someone with a "good personality"...but not much else. But God wants us to be thrilled and fully devoted to the ones we marry. His desires for us are much greater and more complete than our own. That's why he can—and should—be trusted.

Sadly, I didn't have confidence in God when I was dating. I was either so desperate to hang on to relationships or so flippant in pursuing them that I embarrassed myself more times than I care to admit. Whether you date, court, or have an arranged marriage, you can trust God's ways because he cares for you.

Some of you may be thinking, *Whoa, Mark! I'm just going on a date, and you're talking about marriage? Slow down, dude.*

While I think it's important to do things with friends of the opposite sex, when it really comes down to it, most people are looking for longer-term relationships. I think we should always take dating very seriously. We need to think purposefully about any people we date with intentions of being "more than friends."

CHAPTER 9

QUALITIES A GIRL SHOULD LOOK FOR IN A GUY

God values certain qualities in people. Those qualities should be important to us, too. Let's take a look at them.

Rather than bury you with a long list of characteristics, let's concentrate on three of the most important ones. If you're serious about honoring the Lord with your dating choices, look for a guy who...

1. SEEKS AFTER GOD

"A man's steps are directed by the Lord. How then can anyone understand his own way?" (Proverbs 20:24). And "There is no wisdom, no insight, no plan that can succeed against the Lord" (Proverbs 21:30).

Enough said? If God isn't a guy's number one priority, then you can't enjoy a meaningful, fulfilling relationship with that guy. And that can be a problem, because there seems to be a shortage of guys who seek after God during their college years. Apparently it takes us guys a little longer to realize our need to depend upon God completely.

While a man who loves God may be hard to come by, make sure you wait until you find one. Without God, your guy will be lost—and he'll probably take you down with him!

2. SHOWS LEADERSHIP QUALITIES

"Wives, submit to your husbands as to the Lord. For the husband is the head of the wife as Christ is the head of the church, his body, of which he is the Savior. Now as the church submits to Christ, so also wives should submit to their husbands in everything. Husbands, love your wives, just as Christ loved the church and gave himself up for her" (Ephesians 5:22-25).

God's design for families is for husbands to assume the leadership position. Guys who are unwilling or unable to lead cannot give you what God has in mind for you. That's also true about guys who confuse leadership with lordship. You're not looking for a control freak. You're looking for a guy who knows where he's going in life—someone you can feel good about submitting to.

I've found that very few women have difficulty submitting to a man who truly loves them the way Christ loves the church. If you don't see that potential in the guys you go out with, keep looking. Find someone who's going someplace you'd be willing to go, too.

3. IS KIND
"A kind man benefits himself, but a cruel man brings trouble on himself'" (Proverbs 11:17).

I know many girls with low self-esteem who allow guys to trash them because they believe a decent guy could never love them. I also know girls who have a thing for guys who are in trouble. The book of Proverbs shows us the relationship between kindness and trouble. If you want to benefit your life, find a kind man. Otherwise, you may find yourself living out an episode of *The Jerry Springer Show.*

CHAPTER 10

QUALITIES A GUY SHOULD LOOK FOR IN A GIRL

If you're serious about making good choices in your dating life, look for a girl who...

1. SEEKS AFTER GOD

"But seek first his kingdom and his righteousness, and all these things will be given to you as well" (Matthew 6:33).

Nothing is more beautiful than a woman who loves God with her whole self. You know your first priority should be to seek God and his will for your life. Your ideal woman, then, is one who shares your passion for God and his work.

The best places to look for such a woman are those spots where God is the central focus—Sunday school classes, Bible study groups, Christian outreach events and volunteer organizations.

The best way to attract a godly woman is to be the kind of godly man she's looking for.

2. POSSESSES A GOOD CHARACTER

In addition to being one of the wisest men in history, Solomon was a world-class ladies' man. Any advice he offers about women deserves our full attention. Here are three nuggets of Solomon's hard-earned relationship wisdom:

> "A wife of noble character is her husband's crown, but a disgraceful wife is like decay in his bones." (Proverbs 12:4)

> "Better to live on a corner of the roof than share a house with a quarrelsome wife." (Proverbs 21:9)

> "A wife of noble character who can find? She is worth far more than rubies." (Proverbs 31:10)

It's not hard to find a woman you enjoy looking at, one who stirs your physical passion. It's not hard to find a woman you enjoy hanging out with, one who shares your interests and sense of humor. But finding a woman whose inner qualities command your respect—one who inspires you and makes you want to be a better person? That's the one you want to hold onto.

Before I proposed to my wife, one of my chief concerns about marriage was whether I'd be able to remain faithful to one person for the rest of my life. And while that's ultimately a matter of my own personal integrity, I must tell you that finding a woman I can treasure has made it much less of a concern to me.

3. POSSESSES INNER BEAUTY

Our culture in the United States focuses far too much on skin-deep beauty.

As a result, many guys are unable to appreciate—or even recognize—a woman's inner beauty because we've been overexposed to so much flesh. One of the greatest threats to our ability to see what really makes a woman beautiful—and therefore one of the greatest obstacles to finding the right woman—is pornography. If you really want to see women the way God made them, you have to focus on their inner selves.

Peter talks about that challenge in 1 Peter 3:3-5: "Your beauty should not come from outward adornment, such as elaborate hairstyles and the wearing of gold jewelry and fine clothes. Rather, it should be that of your inner self, the unfading beauty of a gentle and quiet spirit, which is of great worth in God's sight. For this is the way the holy women of the past who put their hope in God used to make themselves beautiful."

"Unfading beauty"—that's what we should be looking for. My wife happens to be beautiful on the outside. But what if she became horribly disfigured? (My wife just loves my "what ifs.") Would I leave her? Absolutely not. I fell in love with her *inner* beauty, and that won't fade.

I had a teacher who'd been badly scarred in an auto accident. When I first saw her, I must admit that I didn't think she was attractive at all. But by the end of the semester, I found her to be quite attractive. Her inner beauty was so great that it overshadowed her physical appearance. That's the quality to look for in the women you date!

CHAPTER 11

VALUING YOUR SEXUAL IDENTITY

No discussion of dating would be complete without a few words about sex and intimacy. Chances are, you're bombarded by sexual information, advice, and images every day. Unfortunately, that bombardment probably has little to do with the kind of sex and intimacy the Creator intended for us.

Don't forget that sex is part of God's creation. He commanded Adam and Eve to be fruitful and multiply (Genesis 1:28), and there's only one way to do that! But God didn't design sex only for the purposes of procreation. He created our bodies so we'd receive intense pleasure from sex. What's more, he encourages us to enjoy it!

Take a look at these words in Proverbs 5:18-20: "May your fountain be blessed, and may you rejoice in the wife of your youth. A loving doe, a graceful deer—may her breasts satisfy you always, may you ever be captivated by her love. Why be captivated, my son, by an adulteress? Why embrace the bosom of another man's wife?"

There's the key: God wants us to enjoy sexual activity, but he wants us to experience it within a marriage relationship. God places tremendous value on the sexual relationship between a husband and a wife—and only in that context.

I don't need to tell you how difficult it is to keep sex in its proper context. I was a virgin when I got married, but my victory was hard-won. I had to work at remaining pure. Let me share four principles that helped me.

1. DECIDE TO WAIT UNTIL MARRIAGE TO HAVE SEX

When it came to eating food that wasn't good for him, "Daniel resolved not to defile himself" (Daniel 1:8). He made a decision not to eat it. Period. In the same way, you need to make a decision that sexual purity is important to you. You need to determine not to defile your body, and then you must take steps to protect that decision.

Whether you're on a date or in a steady relationship, making it clear that sex is not an activity you want to participate in at this stage in your life will go a long way toward helping you win the battle against temptation.

2. WATCH YOUR ENVIRONMENT

In the seventh chapter of Proverbs, Solomon describes a scene in which a man is ensnared by an adulterous woman. The man's first mistake is putting himself in the wrong place at the wrong time. The woman's husband is away. Her bed is sprinkled with perfumes and spices. The mood is right for love. The question is, *Why did the guy put himself in such a position?*

The same question applies to anyone who gives sexual temptation a foothold. For many people, sexual urges are difficult to battle under the *best* circumstances. When you add to the mix a sexually charged environment or a convenient opportunity, you're just asking for trouble.

While we were engaged, my wife was still a college student. She had an apartment to herself, and this meant we had to set some very specific boundaries regarding how we spent our time together. There were just too many opportunities available to us, and we couldn't treat them lightly. (If you think waiting for marriage is difficult when you're dating, imagine the pressure you experience when you're engaged!)

For example, I knew that the later in the day we were together, the harder it would be for us to stay pure. As I left my fiancé's apartment one evening, one of her friends saw me leave. She was shocked that I wasn't sleeping over. In fact, she was amazed by the boundaries we'd set because she'd assumed we were already sexually active.

Drinking alcohol is notorious for lowering people's inhibitions and creating tempting sexual opportunities. Regardless of what your beliefs are regarding Christians and alcohol, you must recognize that your judgment can be impaired after only a few drinks. Choosing not to drink is only one step. If others are drinking, you still need to be on guard. When they're under the influence of alcohol, guys can become more aggressive, and girls can become more seductive. So be careful and watch your environment.

3. REALIZE THAT YOU'RE WEAK

In addition to making sure you're not in the wrong place at the wrong time, you have to be aware of what you're doing when you're together. King David, whom the Bible describes as a man after God's heart (Acts 13:22), was relaxing on the roof of his palace one night when he spotted a young woman taking a bath. David had faced giants, wild beasts, and enemy armies—and won. He wrote some of the most famous passages in Scripture. His reputation was spotless. So resisting a little sexual temptation should have been no problem for him.

But David didn't resist. He gave in to his curiosity and lust. He sent for the female bather, whose name was Bathsheba, and the two of them began a sexual affair. And David did all of this despite the fact that she was married to one of his best soldiers. The sex led to Bathsheba's pregnancy, which led to a cover up, which led to murder, which led to the death of David and Bathsheba's newborn son. All of this pain for just a few minutes of passion.

If the mighty King David could become weak enough to make a bad decision in the heat of the moment, then so can you and I. Of all the things that helped me wait until marriage, realizing my own weakness probably made the biggest difference. I realized that just because I was a minister and just because I'd made a decision to wait, that didn't mean I'd be able to resist if I were tempted. So I was very careful to avoid tempting situations. I never allowed myself to believe I was invincible. (Isn't there a proverb that says pride comes before a fall? See Proverbs 16:18-19.)

Philippians 4:13 assures us that in our weakness we can rely on God's strength because he'll give us what we need to make it through.

4. LOOK FOR A WAY OUT

In his first letter to the Corinthians, Paul assures his readers that any temptation we face is common to human experience and that when we're tempted, God will provide a way of escape (see 1 Corinthians 10:13). Our job is to find the escape route God provides.

One of the first places to look is in the experiences of others. The fact is, you probably know a lot of people who've faced the same kinds of temptations you're facing. Talk to some trusted, mature Christian friends. Find out what they did to avoid and overcome temptation.

And God promises that he won't allow us to face a temptation we can't resist. That leaves us with no excuse.

We can't cop out and say a situation was too overwhelming to resist. A guy once told me that everyone in his family had strong sex drives, so he couldn't help but have sex. I laughed and said, "Yeah, you and just about every family I know!" God promises an escape route in every situation. We just need to recognize it.

An escape route could be anything that breaks temptation's spell—the ring of a telephone, a walk around the block, or getting out of the car. I had my own method for breaking temptation's spell among the teenagers in my area. I called it "lustbusting." Armed with my trusty, high-powered halogen flashlight, I'd take small groups of students (often freshmen) through parking lots late at night, and we'd look for wayward couples who were spending too much time together in parked cars. When the moment was right, we'd all point our flashlights at the car and then turn them on. Talk about a mood killer! I wasn't trying to embarrass anyone. I did it for fun. But looking back on it now, I realize God may have used my mischief for good!

Remember, there are two ways to gain wisdom: The easy way, through observation and obedience, and the hard way, through our own mistakes. Regardless of how you got your wisdom, you can put it to good use and guard your sexual purity from this point on.

DON'T UNDERESTIMATE THE IMPACT OF SEXUAL SIN

Now that we've talked about preventative measures for maintaining your sexual purity, there's a tough question we need to tackle: What do you do if you've already given in to sexual temptation? Your first job should be to read 1 John 1:9. If you're genuinely sorry about what you've done, God will forgive you.

Paul warns in Romans 6:1-2 that God's willingness to forgive doesn't give us a free pass to sin. True repentance involves turning your back on sin and moving away from it. It's important to seek God's forgiveness because once you have it, then you can begin to move on with your life.

I've met many guys and girls who consider themselves "damaged goods" because they went too far sexually. They wonder how anyone, including God, could ever love them. The shame they carry is almost unbearable. For some, the guilt leads to a downward spiral of self-destruction. Girls convince themselves that no decent guy will ever want them, so they allow indecent guys to use them. Other girls try to deny their feelings, and they end up shutting down very real emotions and hurts. The end result is often bitterness and depression. Guys can feel shame, too. They may react similarly to girls, continuing to wreck their lives because they feel they have nothing more to lose.

Don't be like them! Ask God for forgiveness and find a mature Christian (of your same gender) whom you can trust with your story—someone who can help guide you through your pain.

CHAPTER 12

FRIENDSHIP CASE STUDIES AND QUESTIONS

I ALREADY HAVE A DATE ON FRIDAY

Nigel, a sophomore in high school, is the son of the family minister at his church. Nigel is part of a group of four male friends who've all grown up in the church.

When a new girl named Violet started attending the youth group, Nigel was smitten. He told his friends he was going to ask her out the following Sunday. However, when Sunday came and Nigel approached Violet, she told him she already had plans to go out with Matt, Nigel's best friend at church—and one of the guys he'd confided in about his interest in Violet.

1. Do boundaries exist in Nigel and Matt's friendship? If so, what are they? If not, what boundaries should exist?

2. How might the wisdom of Proverbs 25:21 ("If your enemy is hungry, give him food to eat; if he is thirsty, give him water to drink") apply to this situation?

3. How might the wisdom of Proverbs 18:17 ("The first to present his case seems right, until another comes forward and questions him") help Nigel and Matt's friendship?

4. How should Nigel approach Matt now? What should he say?

5. How might the wisdom of Proverbs 17:9 ("He who covers over an offense promotes love, but whoever repeats the matter separates close friends") help Nigel approach Matt?

DON'T MIND ME

Vicki and Hannah have been best friends since they started PATH (a program that brings together home-schooled students once a week) when they were in ninth grade. When the two girls first began their friendship, Vicki would invite Hannah to spend the night on weekends and vice versa. They'd also make plans to do their homework together on weeknights.

Over time their friendship became more casual, and they stopped scheduling time together. Instead, Hannah would just pop in at Vicki's house whenever she saw Vicki's mom's car in the driveway. (The girls lived only six blocks apart.) Hannah also expected Vicki to be available to hang out on the weekends.

Now, at the end of their sophomore year, Vicki is tired of Hannah's over-bearing behavior. But since Vicki has never mentioned her frustrations during the two years they've been friends, she doesn't know how to bring it up with Hannah now.

But today was the last straw. While Vicki's mom was still teaching Vicki and her siblings, Hannah walked into the house and said, "Don't mind me," flopped down on the couch, and clicked on the television.

1. How might the wisdom of Proverbs 25:17 ("Seldom set foot in your neighbor's house—too much of you, and he will hate you") help Vicki and Hannah's friendship?

2. Do you think Hannah respects Vicki? Do you think Vicki respects Hannah? Explain.

3. How should Vicki approach Hannah about the situation? What should she say?

4. What boundaries should the girls set? How might that help their friendship?

5. What should Vicki have said when Hannah walked into the house uninvited?

EASILY ANGERED

Even though they come from radically different family backgrounds, David, Sean, and Chris have started hanging out together on weekends.

David's parents are happily married, and his family attends church together every Sunday.

Sean lives with his single mom who divorced Sean's dad when Sean was four. For as long as Sean can remember, it's been just him and his mother. They regularly attend church together.

Chris lives with his mom and her boyfriend Carl. Chris's mom attends church once every few weeks—without Carl or Chris. Carl is the third boyfriend Chris can remember, and he's been around the longest. Chris and Carl are always yelling at each other about how poorly the other one treats Chris's mom.

Sean invites David and Chris over for the weekend. They pitch a tent in Sean's backyard; and later that night, the three of them start talking about religion. When Sean says something that offends Chris, they start arguing. In the middle of the argument, Chris picks up a halogen lantern and throws it against the wooden fence.

1. How might the wisdom of Proverbs 22:24-25 ("Do not make friends with a hot-tempered man, do not associate with one easily angered, or you may learn his ways and get yourself ensnared.") play out in the friendship of David, Sean, and Chris?

2. Can David, Sean, and Chris's friendship continue? Why or why not? And if so, how should it proceed from here?

3. How should David and Sean respond to Chris's outburst?

4. If Chris understood Proverbs 11:17 ("A kind man benefits himself, but a cruel man brings trouble on himself"), how might he act differently?

5. What should Chris do?

YOU DIDN'T HEAR IT FROM ME

Gwen, a junior in high school, is the junior captain of the drill team and a student leader in her youth group. Stacey is also a junior, and she just moved to the area at the beginning of the semester. Stacey is bright, bubbly, and beautiful. She loves people, and she's made quite a few friends at her new school. Some of her new friends are also Gwen's friends. In fact, when Gwen called her best friend about doing something on Friday night, she found out that her friend was already out with Stacey. Rather than getting angry, Gwen decided that Stacey would make a great addition to her group of friends.

On Monday, Gwen spots Stacey in the lunchroom and invites her to sit with Gwen and her friends. Stacey is delighted. As she sits down, she hears the conversation at the table and immediately chimes in with some embarrassing information about the people being discussed. Stacey reveals things that no one else at the table knows. When someone tries to point out that what Stacey is saying is none of their business, Stacey just smiles and says, "Oh, I know. But you didn't hear it from me."

1. How might the wisdom of Proverbs 20:19 ("A gossip betrays a confidence; so avoid a man who talks too much.") help Stacey? How might it help Gwen deal with the situation?

2. Should Gwen pull Stacey aside and say something about her gossiping? If so, when would be a good time and what should she say? If not, why?

3. How might the wisdom of Proverbs 17:9 ("He who covers over an offense promotes love, but whoever repeats the matter separates close friends") help the friendships in this situation?

4. How might the wisdom of Proverbs 27:6 ("Wounds from a friend can be trusted, but an enemy multiplies kisses.") apply to this situation?

5. In what ways could Gwen help Stacey?

OOPS...I DID IT AGAIN

Parker and Wayne are seniors in high school and best friends. They attend the same church, and they've spent four years in youth group together. Parker is president of the science honors society and a varsity swimmer. He also works part-time as a runner at a local hospital. Wayne is the leading receiver on the varsity football team. He makes straight A's, and he's a National Merit Scholar.

Recently, Parker hasn't been able to hang out with Wayne much on the weekends because of his job at the hospital. So Wayne has started going out with some guys from the football team instead. Parker has heard that Wayne and his new buddies have been drinking on Friday and Saturday nights. When Parker asks Wayne about it, Wayne seems extremely regretful.

"I don't want to do it," he explains, "but the other guys love to drink, so I go along with them." Wayne confesses that he's gotten drunk several times, but he promises he won't do it again. The next weekend Parker has to work on Saturday night, so Wayne goes out with his football buddies. In Sunday school the next morning, Parker can tell that Wayne is hung over.

1. How might the wisdom of Proverbs 26:11 ("As a dog returns to its vomit, so a fool repeats his folly.") apply to this situation?

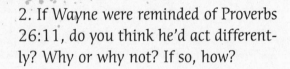

2. If Wayne were reminded of Proverbs 26:11, do you think he'd act differently? Why or why not? If so, how?

3. What should Parker do now? What should his attitude be toward the friendship?

4. Do you think Parker respects Wayne? Do you think Wayne respects Parker? Explain.

5. How could the principle of Proverbs 22:1 ("A good name is more desirable than great riches; to be esteemed is better than silver or gold.") change the dynamics of Parker and Wayne's friendship?

IS THAT TRUE?

Vicki and Gail are both first-borns and highly esteemed students in their junior class. They attend youth group together. In fact, Vicki and Gail grew up together, and their moms are also best friends. Vicki and Gail are the kind of friends who tell each other everything. Or so one of them thought.

Lately, Gail has noticed that Vicki seems distant. She's been pulling away for some reason, and she doesn't come to youth group as regularly as she used to. Gail is concerned.

Vicki and Gail attend different Wednesday night Area Bible Studies (ABS). One Wednesday night, Vicki pulls aside one of her ABS leaders and admits to her that she has an eating disorder. The leader hugs Vicki, and she assures Vicki that she loves her. Later that night, the leader takes the proper measures by telling the youth pastor what happened. Together, with the assistance of Vicki's parents, they work to get Vicki the help she needs.

A week later, Gail finds out from another student that Vicki has an eating disorder. Gail tells the student to stop spreading rumors.

"Vicki tells me everything," Gail says. "If she had an eating disorder, I'd know it." Eventually, Gail asks Vicki about the rumor, and Vicki admits that it's true.

1. How might the wisdom of Proverbs 27:6 ("Wounds from a friend can be trusted, but an enemy multiples kisses.") apply to this situation?

2. What should Gail do?

3. How might the truth of Proverbs 27:17 ("As iron sharpens iron, so one man sharpens another.") help Vicki and Gail's friendship?

4. Do you think Vicki respects Gail? Do you think Gail respects Vicki? Explain.

5. How might the wisdom of Proverbs 18:24 ("A man of many companions may come to ruin, but there is a friend who sticks closer than a brother.") apply to Vicki and Gail's situation?

DON'T YOU THINK I LOOK HOT?

Diana, a freshman in high school, went to the mall with her mom. Diana's mom gave Diana a wad of cash and told her she could buy whatever she wanted. Her mom then left to get a full spa treatment. Diana didn't need to be told twice. She hit all of her favorite stores; and in no time at all, she'd spent every dollar her mom had given to her. She loved the clothes she'd bought, and she couldn't wait to wear them.

That Thursday night at her Area Bible Study, Diana told her leader and the girls in the group about her shopping spree. They all wanted to see her new stuff, so Diana skipped to her room to change into some of the clothes she'd bought.

Her first outfit brought coos from the group. The leader hesitated a little, thinking Diana's skirt was a bit short. But she didn't say anything. When

Diana came out in her third outfit, though, even Diana's best friend, MJ, was uncomfortable. Diana was wearing a low-cut shirt, an extremely short skirt, and boots that came up to her thighs.

1. How might MJ use the words of Proverbs 11:22 ("Like a gold ring in a pig's snout is a beautiful woman who shows no discretion.") to confront Diana?

2. Do you think MJ should say something to Diana about her clothing? If so, what? If not, why?

3. How do the words of Proverbs 27:17 ("As iron sharpens iron, so one man sharpens another.") apply to this situation—particularly to MJ's responsibility to Diana?

4. What could the small group do, in terms of friendship, for Diana? For MJ?

5. Whose responsibility is greater when it comes to talking to Diana about her clothing: MJ, the entire small group, or the group's leader? Why?

IT WAS LIKE THAT

For his sixteenth birthday, Jacob's parents bought him a 2008, soft-top, jet-black, two-door Jeep. Two weeks later, on the first weekend of summer, Jacob invited three of his closest friends—Shea, Andrew, and Zach—to meet him at his grandpa's farm to go off-roading.

The boys had been to the farm many times, so when Jacob arrived, he left the gate open for them. Then he parked his brand-new Jeep in front of his grandpa's house and went in to say hi. After about 20 minutes, Shea showed up. A few minutes later, Andrew arrived. About 10 minutes after that, Zach appeared.

After the boys finished talking to Jacob's grandpa, they all went outside to take the Jeep for a ride. That's when Jacob spotted a huge dent in the side of his new vehicle.

Immediately he looked at all of the other vehicles in the driveway. Each was parked at least 10 feet away from the Jeep.

Zach broke the silence, "I'm sorry, Jacob," he said. "I saw that dent when I got here. I thought you knew it was like that."

Andrew said, "Me too, Jacob. It was like that when I got here."

Shea looked at the three of them and said, "What? It wasn't me. I didn't see it when I got here."

1. How do the words of Proverbs 18:17 ("The first to present his case seems right, till another comes forward and questions him") apply to this situation?

2. What should Jacob do now? Why?

3. How might this situation affect the friendship between Jacob and the other three boys? Why?

4. How might this situation affect the friendships between Shea, Andrew, and Zach? Why?

5. Do you think Shea, Andrew, and Zach respect Jacob? Do you think Shea, Andrew, and Zach respect each other? Explain.

YOU'RE STEALING HIM AWAY FROM ME

Quentin and Bill have been best friends since preschool. Now juniors, they both attend the same high school. Quentin grew up in the church. Bill didn't. Quentin has tried to talk to Bill about Jesus several times. But Bill has repeatedly explained to Quentin that he "doesn't need all that religion."

Bill recently made another friend, Vince. Bill and Vince met at a golf tournament, and they quickly became good friends. Bill told Quentin all about Vince, and he told Vince all about Quentin. When Quentin and Vince finally met, they hit it off right away. They hit it off so well, in fact, that they started hanging out without Bill sometimes.

One day Quentin talked to Vince about Jesus. Vince accepted Jesus on the spot and started going to church with Quentin. When Bill found out about it, he got very angry and stopped talking to both Quentin and Vince.

1. How might the wisdom of Proverbs 27:17 ("As iron sharpens iron, so one man sharpens another.") apply to this situation?

2. Why do you think Bill is angry with Quentin and Vince?

3. How should each guy deal with the situation? What are the guys' responsibilities to one another?

4. Do you think Vince and Quentin betrayed Bill? If so, how? If not, why?

5. How might the wisdom of Proverbs 18:17 ("The first to present his case seems right, till another comes forward and questions him") apply to this situation?

YOU'RE LIKE A BROTHER TO ME

Steven and Laura, two seniors in high school, have been dating for almost a year. They've professed their undying love for one another and talked about getting married after graduation. Steven's best friend, Jack, who's also a senior, introduced the two lovebirds.

Laura and Jack have known each other since sixth grade. Steven and Jack have known each other since preschool. The fact that Jack and Laura occasionally hung out together made Steven suspicious at first. But both Laura and Jack have assured Steven that nothing is going on between them.

In fact, Jack looked Steven squarely in the eye and said, "Do you think I'd ever do something like that to you? You're like a brother to me!" That ended Steven's suspicions.

Today, on their one-year anniversary, Steven decides he wants to surprise Laura by delivering a dozen red roses to her house—unannounced! Sneaking in the back door, he sees Jack and Laura lip-locked on the couch.

1. How might the words of Proverbs 18:17 ("The first to present his case seems right, till another comes forward and questions him") apply to this situation?

2. Do you think Jack respects Steven? Explain.

3. How might the advice of Proverbs 17:9 ("He who covers over an offense promotes love, but whoever repeats the matter separates close friends") apply to this situation?

4. What should Jack do in this situation? What should Steven do?

5. How do you think Jack and Steven's friendship will play out? Why?

6. If they thought about the words of Proverbs 25:21 ("If your enemy is hungry, give him food to eat; if he is thirsty, give him water to drink"), do you think their friendship would play out differently? Explain.

Ecclesiastes is about a king who tried everything and came to a radical conclusion about how life should be lived.

Living a Life That Matters helps you make sense of Solomon's experiences, leads you to meaning in your own life, and gives you the tools to help your friends do the same.

Living a Life That Matters
Lessons from Solomon—the Man Who Tried Everything
Mark Matlock
RETAIL $9.99
ISBN 0-310-25816-2

Visit www.invertbooks.com or your local bookstore.

Movies and TV programs that glorify witchcraft and occult practices are sucking teenagers just like you into a web of lies. This book draws a clear distinction between what's real and what's not; what the Bible says, and what it doesn't say when it comes to the supernatural.

Don't Buy the Lie
Discerning Truth in a World of Deception
Mark Matlock
RETAIL $9.99
ISBN 0-310-25814-6

Visit www.invertbooks.com or your local bookstore.

Many people think teenagers aren't capable of much. But Zach Hunter is proving those people wrong. He's only fifteen, but he's working to end slavery in the world—and he's making changes that affect millions of people. Find out how Zach is making a difference and how you can make changes in the things that you see wrong with our world.

Be the Change
Your Guide to Freeing Slaves and Changing the World
Zach Hunter
RETAIL $9.99
ISBN 0-310-27756-6

Visit www.invertbooks.com or your local bookstore.

Love This! contains real-life stories of people like you who've found ways to love their neighbors. It will challenge you to make a difference in your world by loving people who are often ignored or unloved—the homeless, the addicted, the elderly, those of different races, even your enemies—and show you tangible ways you can demonstrate that love.

Love This!
Learning to Make It a Way of Life, Not Just a Word
Andy Braner
RETAIL $12.99
ISBN 0-310-27380-3

Visit www.invertbooks.com or your local bookstore.

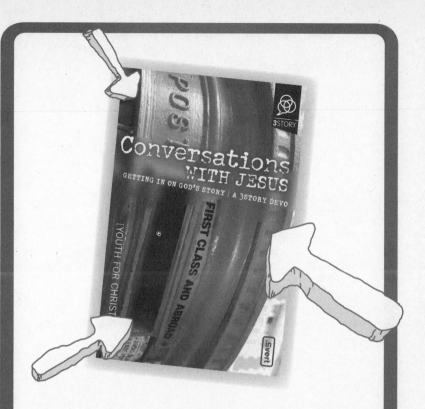

Listen to what Jesus has to say to you. In this 60-day devo
you'll receive daily letters from Jesus and spend some time
journaling your thoughts back to him as you take part in the
conversation.

Conversations with Jesus
Getting in on God's Story
Youth for Christ
RETAIL $10.99
ISBN 0-310-27346-3

If you've ever wondered if God is really there and listening, if you're good enough, or what's so great about heaven, you're not alone. We all have had personal questions, but the answers are often harder to come by. In this book, you'll discover how to navigate your big questions, and what the answers mean for your life and faith.

Living with Questions
Dale Fincher
RETAIL $9.99
ISBN 0-310-27664-0

Visit www.invertbooks.com or your local bookstore.

You know that being a student leader is no small task—nor is it something to lose sleep over. If you have student leaders—or at least students who are willing to lead—use this book to pair their willingness with tools and techniques to create effective leaders who lighten your load.

Help! I'm a Student Leader!
Practical Ideas and Guidance on Leadership
Doug Fields
RETAIL $9.99
ISBN 0-310-25961-4

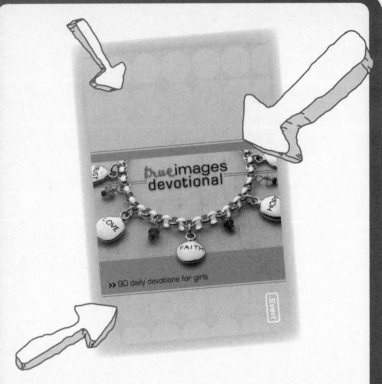

What is true beauty? Learn what it means to develop lasting inner beauty, the kind that God desires for you! By spending time in God's Word each day, you'll understand more about being the beautiful young woman God created you to be. Each devotion contains a Bible verse, a thought for the day, further reading, a prayer, and space to journal your thoughts.

True Images Devotional
90 Daily Devotionals for Girls
RETAIL $12.99
ISBN 0-310-26705-6